FACING YOUR
GIANTS

BUDDY **CRABTREE**

Facing Your Giants

Introduction

A small, overlooked shepherd boy, wearing nothing but his regular ragged clothing, was standing face to face with a nine-foot-tall giant who was wearing the finest armor and wielding a sword that probably weighed just as much as the boy. Everyone's heart was racing. An entire army stood behind the giant laughing in confidence. The army on the other side stood trembling in fear and wetting their chainmail.

The boy raised a smooth stone and in a matter of seconds the giant, who was called Goliath, was face down in the dirt. The boy ran over, grabbed the sword and cut off the giant's head.

Everyone was silent. Did this just really happen? The most incapable, unknown, weak, and worthless shepherd boy just slayed the most feared giant in the land. How can that be possible?

The shepherd boy realized that he had nothing to fear whatsoever. Why is that? He knew that this giant wasn't opposing him, his land, or his people. That giant was opposing God. The small shepherd boy knew that nobody who stood against his God would be standing very long.

> **Nobody who stands against our God Will be standing for very long.**

Put yourself in the shepherd boy's shoes. You're standing in front of a massive giant who wants nothing more for you than to paralyze you in fear and anxiety. What do you do? Freeze, run, or fight?

We all face giants in our lifetimes: anxiety, depression, habitual sins, broken homes, broken lives, addictions, etc. That giant isn't really out to get you. He's out to get your God. Since he knows he can't touch God, he'll do what he can to mess with those that God loves most, his people. YOU!

Do you know the power that is really on your side? Do you see that the God standing behind you is far greater than any giant standing in front of you? When you realize the power and authority that comes when God is with you, you will gain the title of Giant Slayer!

Romans 8:30-31 says, "And those whom he predestined he also called, and those whom he called he also justified, and those whom he justified he also glorified. What then shall we say to these things? If God is for us, who can be against us?"

I want you to remember something before you begin reading this book. No words of mine will change you. No book, no sermon, nor preacher can really mold you into a giant slayer. Only the pursuit of an active relationship with God can. Let this book guide you. Let God transform you!

Day 1
Changing Your Perspective

1 Samuel 17:45-47 (ESV)
David said to the Philistine (Goliath), "You have come against me with sword and spear and javelin, but I come against you in the name of the LORD Almighty, the God of the armies of Israel, whom you have defied. This day the LORD will deliver you into my hand, and I will strike you down and cut off your head. And I will give the dead bodies of the host of the Philistines this day to the birds of the air and to the wild beasts of the earth, that all the earth may know that there is a God in Israel, and that all this assembly may know that the LORD saves not with sword and spear. For the battle is the LORD's, and he will give you into our hand."

These were some strong words coming from a little dude. I mean, when you read the whole story, you see an entire army crippled in fear of this one man—one giant. Every individual saw the giant, but nobody had a clue how to face him. They were crippled in fear because of him.

We all have our giants. Thousands of people have experienced their crippling effects. When he comes around, you're paralyzed, maybe even without warning; terrified, sometimes without any cause. But just like Goliath, any giant has the potential to fall.

You have to remember that you have a "gianter" God (I totally just made up that word, but I'm keeping it). Your giants might not go away in a day. Through time of seeking that gianter God and understanding that he is for you all the way, reminding yourself consistently of His love and protection over you, and knowing that He desires peace and calmness for you, you can find that the your giant takes a back seat in your life. He would rather not encounter you and your big big God.

> **When God takes an active role in your life, your giants take a back seat.**

Realize that David didn't become a giant slayer on accident; he dedicated his life to worshipping God, understanding His strength, and killing smaller giants along the way.

I know that it's easy to come to a point where fighting this giant seems pointless. I struggled with depression for most of my life and I reached a point where I just accepted it. I now realize that this was an opportunity for me to see that there is a God in my life who can use me and empower me despite my depression. The more I realized that, the more it became an afterthought in my life. Just as David said, "and the whole world will know that there is a God in Israel. All those gathered here will know that it is not by sword or spear that the Lord saves; for the battle is the LORD's, and he will give all of you into our hands."

He knew His God. The rest of the Israelite army didn't. They accepted their fate; you don't have to accept yours. I pray that this journey will be your opportunity to face that giant and let the world know that the battle you're trying to fight isn't yours to fight alone, but God's. You just have to step onto that battlefield and throw the first stone.

Reflection:
Take some time today seeking God and praying that he shows you just an ounce of his "giantness" (another word I made up). He can do all things, and He wants to help you fight this giant. "And surely I am with you always, to the very end of the age." Matthew 28:20

Day 2
Living in Denial

Matthew 16:24-26 (NIV)
*"Then Jesus said to his disciples, 'Whoever wants
to be my disciple must deny themselves and take up
their cross and follow me. For whoever wants to
save their life will lose it, but whoever loses their
life for me will find it. What good will it be for
someone to gain the whole world, yet forfeit their
soul? Or what can anyone give in exchange for
their soul?"*

Jesus didn't go to the cross so that you could better
yourself. He went to the cross so you could become
less of yourself and more like Him. To be honest, this
isn't a self-help book. My job isn't to guide you into
becoming a better you. That was never the idea of
Scripture. The journey of overcoming giants does not
come through you becoming greater, but becoming
less.

> **Jesus didn't go to the cross so you
> could better yourself, but become less
> of yourself and more like Him.**

Paul tells us in Galatians 2:20, "For I have been
crucified with Christ. Therefore, I no longer live, but
Christ lives in me. The life I now live, I live in faith
in the Son of God who loved me and gave himself for

me." This passage reminds us that the Christian life is a life where we live out this reality: I don't live for myself anymore. Ask yourself this question, "What did I lay on that cross: my sins, or my sinful self?" It's very easy to say, "God, take away my sin and my guilt." It's far more difficult to say, "God, take all of me and give me more of you." I can tell you, if you only throw your sins on that cross in an attempt to feel less guilt, you'll find yourself doing the same thing over and over, wondering why you haven't found hope and restoration from the cross. You can't join Christ in His glorious resurrection, unless you first join Him in His death.

Understand, when Jesus died on that cross, He knew that this was the only way for us to receive not a better life, but a new life. 1 Corinthians 5:14-17 tells us, *"For Christ's love compels us, because we are convinced that one died for all, and therefore all died. And he died for all, that those who live should no longer live for themselves but for him who died for them and was raised again. So from now on we regard no one from a worldly point of view. Though we once regarded Christ in this way, we do so no longer. Therefore, if anyone is in Christ, the new creation has come: The old has gone, the new is here!"*

This passage speaks for itself. Christ died for all. That includes you! Why? So that you would no longer live for yourself. What happened on the cross happened to allow you to live for God in holiness and purity, free from all sin. That is our purpose. It's our humanity that is constantly pulling us from God. Why would we want to live trying to better our humanity? Jesus went to the cross so that you could become less of yourself and more like him: a holy, righteous, redeemed, blameless, beautiful, and bright child of your incredible God!

Reflection:
Have you ever taken the most important step of your life? Have you confessed your sins to God and fully devoted to spend your life for Him? Have you denied yourself and carried your cross with your Savior? This is your opportunity to cast, not your sins, but your old sinful self to the cross and let God give you NEW life! Confess your sins to God and He will forgive you. Deny yourself and live for Him!

Where in your life do you need to do some denying of yourself and picking up your cross: your relationships, your work, your time, your money, your worries, your entire life? Give it up to God and see what He does with it!

Day 3
Renewed

Romans 12:1-2 (NIV)
*"Therefore, I urge you, brothers and sisters, in
view of God's mercy, to offer your bodies as a
living sacrifice, holy and pleasing to God—this is
your true and proper worship. Do not conform to
the pattern of this world, but be transformed by
the renewing of your mind. Then you will be able
to test and approve what God's will is—his good,
pleasing and perfect will."*

Have you ever found yourself trying to fit into a
mold? Have you ever caught yourself trying to be
someone that you weren't? Can I tell you something
encouraging? You don't have to change who you are
to become a giant slayer. Giant slaying is already in
you! That same power that conquered the grave is in
you. You don't have to try to change yourself. You
don't have to conform to a mold. All you have to do
is allow God to transform your mind!

This is one of my favorite passages, but it is often
misinterpreted. Here's what it doesn't say: "Do not
conform to the pattern of this world, but conform to
the pattern of the church." Many preachers teach, "Do
not conform to the pattern of this world, but conform
to the pattern that I tell you to conform to." There's
no freedom in that! My purpose as a pastor is not to
try to push you into fitting another mold. My purpose

is to point you into the direction of the only One who can transform your mind. When He transforms your mind, He transforms your heart. When He transforms your heart, He transforms your entire life.

The journey of slaying giants begins with allowing God to transform your mind and the way that you think. When you think you're a failure, you will always be a failure. When you think you're a victor, you will always find victory, even in the moments that seem like defeat.

> **When God transforms your mind, He transforms your entire life.**

The direction of your thoughts is ultimately the direction that you walk. Show me the thoughts you have about yourself and I will show you where you will be ten years from now. Some of the most important thoughts that you think are the thoughts that you think about yourself.

You know, when God looks at a redeemed child, he sees beauty, righteousness, strength, and hope. He sees a victor, a light, a vessel that he can use to tear up giants. Try to see yourself through the eyes of a God who loved you enough to sacrifice his son so that he could see you spotless. Before you can fight the battle against the giants, you need to fight the battle that goes on in your own mind.

Reflection:

Take some time to see yourself through the eyes of God. Realize that even in your failures, God is not in the business of rubbing your nose in your past mistakes. He is holding his hand out to you saying, "Walk with me and I'll take you places that you never thought you could go."

Day 4
Mirror Talk

Proverbs 18:21 (ESV)
"Death and life are in the power of the tongue and those who love it will eat its fruits."

Ephesians 4:29 (ESV)
"Let no corrupting talk come out of your mouths, but only such as is good for building up, as fits the occasion, that it may give grace to those who hear."

Genesis 1:3 (ESV)
"And God said, "Let there be light," and there was light."

Right from the beginning of time, God showed us the power that comes through words. The very first words that he spoke had the power to create all that exists, and all that is. God used words to create the world we live in. Also, by his words he has the ability to end it all as well.

This is such an incredible thought to conceive. What's even more incredible is that God has given us the ability to use words ourselves. Our words are not just a flip of the tongue, but they too hold tremendous power! As the passage in Proverbs says, "Death and life are in the power of the tongue." You've probably heard it said that your words can be used to lift others up or tear them down. I want to tell you that it is exactly the same with the words that we say about ourselves.

I want you to do something for me. Drop this book and take a good long look at yourself in the mirror. I'm totally serious. Do it.

If you didn't do it, don't be a bum and go do it. If you did do it, you're awesome.

Now, what thoughts went through your mind as you looked at the person in the mirror? Were you filled with joy? Hate? Thanksgiving? Bitterness? Hope? Dread? Indifference? What kind of thoughts did you have toward yourself?

The person that you see in that mirror is a direct reflection of the things that you speak about yourself. You see a failure in the mirror because you call yourself a failure. You see a mistake only because you've convinced yourself that you're a mistake.

> **The person that you see in the mirror**
> **Is a direct reflection of the things that you**
> **speak about yourself.**

Nine times out of ten, our giants that we face in life are not the things that we see, do, or feel, but they are the person that we see in the mirror. There are two types of people in this world: those who define themselves by the things that they do and those who define themselves through the eyes of God.

Most people in this world identify themselves either by their accomplishments or their mistakes. Let me tell you, a true giant slayer is born the moment he realizes that his accomplishments don't define him, but his God does.

How does God define you?
- His Child (John 1:12-13)
- Brand New (1 Cor. 5:16-17)
- Free (John 8:32)
- Righteous (2 Cor 5:21)
- His workmanship (Eph. 2:10)
- And so many more incredible things!

Reflection:

Take a long look in the mirror again and call yourself by a new name—a name that isn't birthed from your accomplishments or your failures, but a name that is birthed in the eyes of the God who created you. Make it a point to use your words to redefine your identity. As Paul says in Romans 8:1-2: "There is now no condemnation in those who are in Christ Jesus because through Christ Jesus the law of the Spirit who gives life has set you free from the law of sin and death." Praise Him for your new identity!

Day 5
Hope in His Promises

2 Corinthians 1:18-22 (NIV)
"But as surely as God is faithful, our message to you is not 'Yes' and 'No.' For the Son of God, Jesus Christ, who was preached among you by us – by me and Silas and Timothy – was not 'Yes' and 'No,' but in him it has always been 'Yes.' For no matter how many promises God has made, they are 'Yes' in Christ. And so through him the 'Amen' is spoken by us to the glory of God. Now it is God who makes both us and you stand firm in Christ. He anointed us, set his seal of ownership on us, and put his Spirit in our hearts as a deposit, guaranteeing what is to come."

I wear a wedding ring on my left hand, as do most all married couples. Why? I don't wear it to remind me that I'm married. I don't wear it to even remind me of my wife. This golden band that wraps around my fourth finger is there as a constant reminder of the promises, of the vows that I have made to my wife on July 2, 2016. This ring is a symbol for me, and for everyone around me, that I fully plan to fulfill and live up to the promises that I have made to my wife.

Did you know that God has given us something to remind us that he fully plans to fulfill all the promises that he has made for us as well? What could it be, but the suffering Son on the cross? Paul tells us in this passage, "For no matter how many promises God has made, they are 'Yes' in Christ." That is the moment that God said, "I do." That is the moment that God fulfilled his every promise to us. That is why we sing praises to Him because he has never, nor will He ever, fail to fulfill His promises to us!

God reminds us multiple times throughout scripture that He is the ultimate promise keeper (Deut. 7:9; Numbers 23:19; Romans 4:20-21; 1 Thess 5:24). Some of God's most incredible promises is the promise to never leave us, to be an ever present help in time of need, to be our refuge and our strength, and to give us a way to live victoriously.

Your were created to live courageously, victoriously, and with surpassing joy! It is a promise from God! No giant will outmatch you, no wave will overtake you, and no obstacle will overrun you.

How many promises of God have you encountered in your life? Remember that God rarely ever fulfills His promises the way that we expect Him to. But He always fulfills them in the way that brings us the most growth and builds up our faith in the process.

Reflection:
Take some time to recall the moments in your life where you felt like all hope was lost. How did God bring everything around for you? What did you learn

the most from that situation? You've seen Him do it before; let's watch Him do it again!

Day 6
Walk in your Weaknesses

1 Samuel 16:11-13 (ESV)
"Then Samuel said to Jesse, 'Are all your sons here?' And he said, 'There remains yet the youngest, but behold, he is keeping the sheep.' And Samuel said to Jesse, 'Send and get him, for we will not sit down till he comes here.' And he sent and brought him in. Now he was ruddy and had beautiful eyes and was handsome. And the Lord said, 'Arise, anoint him, for this is he.' Then Samuel took the horn of oil and anointed him in the midst of his brothers. And the Spirit of the Lord rushed upon David from that day forward."

Overcomers are often overlooked. Giant slayers never start out as giant slayers. David is the perfect example of this. Samuel was looking for a king in the house of Jesse. Jesse presented to Samuel "all" of his sons. Actually, he showed him all of his strong, capable, and qualified sons. David was overlooked. How could a quiet shepherd boy who plays his guitar all day ever become anything great?

Verse 7 says it all. As Samuel was looking at David's brothers, "the Lord said to Samuel, 'Do not look on his appearance or on the height of his stature, because I have rejected him. For the Lord sees not as man sees: man looks on the outward appearance, but the Lord looks on the heart.'"

How could we ever become anything great when it seams like our weaknesses rule over our strengths? God doesn't look at our weaknesses or our strengths; he looks at our hearts. Our God doesn't look for people who are able to do great things; he looks for people who are willing to do great things through Him.

Here's something to thank God for today: your weaknesses do not disqualify you from being used by God; they qualify you. It is through those weaknesses that God makes his strength known. This is what Paul was talking about in 2 Cor. 12:9 when he said, "But he said to me, 'My grace is sufficient for you, for my power is made perfect in weakness.' Therefore I will boast all the more gladly of my weaknesses, so that the power of Christ may rest upon me." He also said in 1 Cor. 1:27, "But God chose what is foolish in the world to shame the wise; God chose what is weak in the world to shame the strong."

> **Your weaknesses don't disqualify you from being used by God; they qualify you**

Never forget that God doesn't call the qualified, He qualifies the called.

You may be thinking to yourself, "How in the world could I ever overcome the giants in my life?" I have a very simple, yet very difficult answer for you. Take your eyes off the giant and turn your eyes to God. The direction of your focus will determine the paths that you take. The more you walk in the direction of your giants, the larger they look. The more you fix your eyes on Jesus, the smaller your giants become. This doesn't come from ourselves. It's solely because our God is greater! That's why we can boast in our weaknesses, because they show God's strength. We can proudly declare that our God is great. He has shown us through our weaknesses that we would never be able to accomplish the impossible without Him.

Reflection:
Don't overlook yourself today. Proudly declare your weaknesses to God and he will show you the real source of your giant-slaying strength. Take some time to thank God for your weaknesses. I know it sounds weird, but always remember that God is growing you, guiding you, and equipping you through those weaknesses so that you can see His strength.

Day 7
Unmet Expectations

John 11:32-37 (NIV)
"When Mary reached the place where Jesus was and saw him, she fell at his feet and said, "Lord, if you had been here, my brother would not have died." When Jesus saw her weeping, and the Jews who had come along with her also weeping, he was deeply moved in spirit and troubled. "Where have you laid him?" he asked. "Come and see, Lord," they replied. Jesus wept. Then the Jews said, "See how he loved him!" But some of them said, "Could not he who opened the eyes of the blind man have kept this man from dying?"

Have you ever been the victim of an unspoken expectation? Has someone ever gotten mad at you because you failed to do something that had never even crossed your mind? It is extremely frustrating for someone to expect something of you that you never promised. Why do we do that with God?

Many of us, myself included, are guilty of having expectations of God that he remains to leave unmet. We become frustrated with Him, even angry and bitter, when He fails to meet our expectations. We pray for healing and deliverance; we see none. We seek God for wisdom and direction, but He is silent. We begin to shout questions to heaven, asking, "Why did you allow this?" "Why didn't you stop that?"

"Why aren't you listening to me?"

The real question that we should all ask is this: am I willing to serve a God who doesn't live up to my expectations? Real faith isn't expecting God to do everything you ask him to do. Real faith is trusting in Him even when He doesn't seem to show up.

> **Are you willing to serve a God who doesn't live up to your expectations?**

This is by far the most difficult devotional for me to write because it sounds like there's a possibility that God doesn't want us to defeat some of our giants. Let me take some time to clarify. God's goal for your life isn't to make you perfect, but to make you holy. Paul had a thorn in his flesh, Moses had a speech impediment, and Elijah dealt with bouts of depression. There will be prayers that will remain unanswered. you will have questions that will never be answered. The good news is that we serve a God whose thoughts are higher than our thoughts, whose ways are higher than our ways. Will you trust a God who doesn't always live up to your expectations?

Mary and Martha both reached out to Jesus when their brother was sick and dying, and He didn't show up until after Lazarus died. The doubt came, then the questions, then the anger. Finally, when Jesus showed up after Lazarus' death, their emotions blew up. "If you had only been here…"

God sees the situation that you are in. He knows what giants are beating you down. But He is NOT sitting up in heaven indifferent to your circumstances. Know that He sees every part of your story from beginning to end. Don't forget that "in all things God works for the good of those who love him, who have been called according to his purpose." Romans 8:28. Your present circumstance is not the end of your story. The pain you are feeling, God feels it too. He is right there weeping with you. He also has a plan for you that is far greater. He has plans to prosper you, not to harm you (Jeremiah 29:11).

Your situation might seem dead. The hope, the trust, the joy might seem like it's buried and lost, just like Lazarus. Remember what Jesus said to these two sisters, "I am the resurrection and the life. The one who believes in me will live, even though they die; and whoever lives by believing in me will never die. Do you believe this?"

Do you believe this? Do you believe that in the midst of the pain, He can bring restoration? In the midst of the questions, He can bring peace. Do you believe that in His incredible knowledge, He might be doing something amazing in you right now? He is! He might leave you with unanswered questions, but He will never leave you.

Reflection:

Take some time to picture God looking over your entire life, from beginning to end. He sees every circumstance, He sees every person impacted by every circumstance, and He knows what will build you into a better you.

Take this time to thank God for the pain and the problems. We rarely grow in times of prosperity. But we can give Him thanks in times of trouble because He is growing us. Silver can't be purified unless it goes through the fire. Steel can never be sharpened until it grinds against stone. God is raising you up to be the ultimate giant destroyer through this!

Day 8
Open Your Eyes

> 2 Kings 6:15-18 (NIV)
> *"When the servant of the man of God got up and went out early the next morning, an army with horses and chariots had surrounded the city. 'Oh no, my lord! What shall we do?' The servant asked. 'Don't be afraid,' the prophet answered. 'Those who are with us are more than those who are with them.' And Elisha prayed, 'Open his eyes, LORD, so that he may see.' Then the LORD opened the servant's eyes, and he looked and saw the hills full of horses and chariots of fire all around Elisha. As the enemy came down toward him, Elisha prayed to the LORD, 'Strike this army with blindness.' So he struck them with blindness, as Elisha had asked."*

This army went after Elisha because of one thing: God used him to help Israel avoid their ambushes and attacks. Elisha was a threat to the enemy because he was close to God, so they went after him.

You are a threat to Satan. Your very relationship with Christ makes him angry. As he is setting up ambushes to attack your friends and family, your relationship with God will interfere with his plans to destroy those you love. Therefore, he comes after you with an army.

Now before you start getting anxious over that

thought, remember what Elisha told his servant! "Don't be afraid," the prophet answered. 'Those who are with us are more than those who are with them." Elisha's servant only saw what his eyes could see. Elisha saw the big picture. His giant God was the one who saw all those men in that army wet their sackcloth as babies. Elisha had nothing to fear, because his giant God was on his side.

> **Those who are with you are far more than those who are against you!**

Nothing can break the attack of the enemy quicker than knowing who your God is and calling on his name as your FIRST line of defense. Any time you feel your giants coming, know that despite the battle going on, the God that is for you is stronger and gianter than anything against you.

Paul said in 2 Corinthians 10:4-5, "For though we live in the world, we do not wage war as the world does. The weapons we fight with are not weapons of this world. On the contrary, they have divine power to demolish strongholds. We demolish arguments and every pretension that sets itself up against the knowledge of God, and we take captive every thought to make it obedient to Christ."

God has the power to come in like a wrecking ball all over those strongholds in your life, scattering those armies. Why? You have an entire army fighting for you. Not just that spiritual army, but you also have family and friends, pastors and leaders all fighting by your side, praying for your success and victory!

There are two types of people in this world: those who see the army against them and those who know the army that is for them. There are those who see the giant, and there are those who see their gianter God. Choose today to see your big God and the army that He has carefully chosen to fight for you.

Reflection:
You are not alone today. Pray that God helps you see the army fighting your battles with you. Find comfort in peace in knowing that he is fighting with you. Thank him for always being there and bringing people in your life that will always have your back!

Day 9
Run

Hebrews 12:1-2 (NIV)
"Therefore, since we are surrounded by such a great cloud of witnesses, let us throw off everything that hinders and the sin that so easily entangles. And let us run with perseverance the race marked out for us, fixing our eyes on Jesus, the pioneer and perfecter of faith. For the joy set before him he endured the cross, scorning its shame, and sat down at the right hand of the throne of God."

I hate running. I despise it with a burning passion deep within my soul. I honestly don't understand how people would even enjoy running. You get sweaty, you get cramps, you can't breathe, you make weird noises, and you don't even get big and buff from it. It's just plain nasty. When my wife and I were still dating, a woman came up to us and said that running is dangerous for our knees since we're short people. From that day on, I have vowed (for the safety of my knees, of course), to never run again.

To be completely honest, I just don't have the patience to get into shape. Becoming an effective runner doesn't happen immediately. It takes weeks, months, and even years to train your body to be able to handle the pressures that come with running. If I told you that, even though I haven't ran since high school, I was planning on running a marathon and getting first place next week, you would think I was crazy. Why do we pick fun at someone who believes they could simply pick themselves up from a life of laziness and run a marathon, yet we beat ourselves up when we are unable to effectively run the race of obedience without training, study, and time?

David, the giant slayer, didn't simply step up one day out of a life of passivity and suddenly defeat the most feared giant of all Philistia. He spent his whole life protecting sheep with his sling. Taking out foxes, then bears, then lions, he was training himself, unknowingly, to become a giant slayer. On top of that, he spent countless hours in the field worshipping and seeking out his God!

If you want to live the life of obedience that God has called you to live, never forget that it is a journey that takes time. You will never wake up one day and suddenly be perfect. Your walk with God goes one step at a time. Defeating small giants at the beginning and building up your endurance every day through your obedience.

Our passage in Hebrews shows us the first step to running the race that God has marked for us to run: "let us throw off everything that hinders and the sin that so easily entangles." It all begins with Christ on the cross. You can't effectively run carrying the weight of your sin. Jesus said in Matthew 11:28-30, "Come to me, all you who are weary and burdened, and I will give you rest. Take my yoke upon you and learn from me, for I am gentle and humble in heart, and you will find rest for your souls. For my yoke is easy and my burden is light." Don't let your regrets, your bitterness, or your past weigh you down. God has something far greater ahead of you.

The next step the writer of Hebrews shows us is, "fix our eyes on Jesus, the pioneer and perfecter of faith." Have you ever looked over your shoulder while walking, running, or driving and noticed when you turned around you veered off course? When you take your eyes off the track, you loose all sense of where you are going. When you take your eyes off of Jesus, your life will veer off track. Don't desire to run the race marked for others. You'll find yourself off the mark that God gave you. Don't look behind you at where you've been. You'll find that you can't see where God is leading you. Don't even look at the people or giants that are standing directly in your path. Fix your eyes solely on your Creator, your Savior, your giant-squashing God. He'll lead you into victory. He'll guide you through the obstacles. Let him build up that endurance in your life! Romans 5:3-4 says, "We can rejoice, too, when we run into problems and trials, for we know that they help us develop endurance. And endurance develops strength of character, and character strengthens our confident hope of salvation."

> **When you take your eyes off Jesus,
> your life will veer off track.**

Galatians 6:9
"So let's not get tired of doing what is good. At just
the right time we will reap a harvest of blessing if we
don't give up."

Reflection
Remember, "we are surrounded by such a great cloud
of witnesses" There's a whole crowd of people
surrounding you, cheering you on as you run this
race. They're watching as you run, as you trip, as you
fall, and as you get back up an keep on running. Take
some time to find out what exactly is hindering you
from running the race that God has marked before
you. Now, turn your eyes upon Jesus. Let his glory
and majesty drown out all your struggles and pain.
Let him guide you and lead you step by step into the
life   that   he   has   prepared   for   you.

Day 10
Don't Worry

Matthew 6:25-34 (NIV)
"Therefore I tell you, do not worry about your life, what you will eat or drink; or about your body, what you will wear. Is not life more than food, and the body more than clothes? Look at the birds of the air; they do not sow or reap or store away in barns, and yet your heavenly Father feeds them. Are you not much more valuable than they? Can any one of you by worrying add a single hour to your life? And why do you worry about clothes? See how the flowers of the field grow. They do not labor or spin. Yet I tell you that not even Solomon in all his splendor was dressed like one of these. If that is how God clothes the grass of the field, which is here today and tomorrow is thrown into the fire, will he not much more clothe you—you of little faith? So do not worry, saying, 'What shall we eat?' or 'What shall we drink?' or 'What shall we wear?' For the pagans run after all these things, and your heavenly Father knows that you need them. But seek first his kingdom and his righteousness, and all these things will be given to you as well. Therefore do not worry about tomorrow, for tomorrow will worry about itself. Each day has enough trouble of its own."

The word "worry" can also be translated as "be anxious." Jesus is literally saying here, "don't be anxious about anything." Now, obviously that's much easier said than done when it feels like the giants you face are beyond your control. That is true. But it's not beyond God's control.

Look at the birds. They don't worry, they're not anxious, they have a God who provides all their needs. All they have to do is sing songs to him all day. I guarantee you that God holds you much higher in value than birds. You are his priority. He loves you and He loves providing for you! Above all, He wants you to know Him and have an intimate relationship with Him!

God is telling you today that he cares about all your worries in your finances, in your family, and in your relationships. Thank God he cares! First Peter 5:7 says, "Cast all your cares on Him because he cares for you." God is not sitting up in heaven indifferent to your struggles; He wants you to pursue Him so He can mold you through them.

Jesus said, "But seek first his kingdom and his righteousness, and all these things will be given to you as well." Without seeking Christ and actively pursuing that necessary relationship with Him wholeheartedly, you will never reap the rewards. It's hard to say this, but this is where the truth comes in to play. The more active your relationship with God is, the more comfort He will bring you. The further you are from Him, the more things you have to worry about. Pursue God in every area of your life, put him first, and rely on him alone, and you will find that peace. The closer and more active you get to God, the bigger he gets in your situations.

You've probably heard this verse before. Philippians 4:6-7 says, "Do not be anxious about anything, but in every situation, by prayer and petition, with thanksgiving, present your requests to God. And the peace of God, which transcends all understanding, will guard your hearts and your minds in Christ Jesus." This is all about relationship. God desires to be close to you always, not just in the hard times. We've all had that friend who is only there for us when they need us, but never when we need them. Don't be that with God. He wants a two-way relationship with you today and everyday. He wants to be closer to you than ever before. Seek Him over the benefits. Give thanks to Him, even when you can't find many reasons to. "Pursue His kingdom and His righteousness and ALL these things will be given to you" (Matthew 6:33). "Delight yourself in the LORD, and he will give you the desires of your heart" (Psalm 37:4).

Reflection:
Write a list of things you are thankful to God for. Take time delighting and thanking Him for what He's doing and for who He is. Ask Him what you can do for Him. Pursue the only God who can do something about your anxiety. He'll bless you for that.

Day 11
The Storm

Picture this incredible scene. Huge waves crashing over a small old fishing boat with a bunch of terrified men in it. The men are frantically grabbing buckets and trying with all their might to get the water out of the boat only for another wave to crash down on top of them, filling the boat again. Tired and exhausted, yet terrified all the same, they keep trying to stay afloat while beaten and bruised by every strong wave that hammers them into the ground. After hours of painstaking work with no results, Peter looks up and shouts, "Where in the world is Jesus?" They run down only to find him snoozing in a puddle of water seeming to be completely unaware of their impending doom. Shaking him awake, they shout at him, "Why are you sleeping? Do you even care that we're all going to die?" Jesus doesn't even say a word. He gets up, walks out to the main deck, and tells the storm to stop it and it actually listened to Him! How incredible is that?

Understand this, so many people today, even Christians, spend so much time and money in a vain attempt to keep from drowning in their lives. The walk around feeling like the water is up past their necks and they don't know what else to do. Just as the disciples spent so much of their time trying to fix their problems on their own, we find ourselves looking for the next home remedy or the greatest DIY trick to relaxation only to find that it only works for a moment and never reaches the source of the issue.

The disciples, in the midst of their panic and anxiety, completely forgot who was in that boat with them. Jesus wasn't scared of the waves because He was God! He was just enjoying the ride, waiting to build relationships with the disciples. They didn't run to him first. They forgot that he was with them. That gave them a lot of unnecessary stress and anxiety.

Check this out: Galatians 2:20 says, "I have been crucified with Christ and I no longer live, but

CHRIST LIVES IN ME. The life I now live in the body, I live by faith in the Son of God, who loved me and gave Himself for me." When you die to yourself and become a Christian, Christ steps into your boat and begins to chill with you. He wants to build that relationship with you. So many Christians forget that He is in their boat with them. Realize that He doesn't always spring into action the second a struggle arises. He's just waiting for you to come to Him in faith.

We add a lot of stress to our lives when Jesus becomes our last resort. We are really good at trying to do things on our own while the entire problem can be solved in coming to Christ for help first. The Bible says, "God is our refuge and strength, a very present help in trouble" (Psalms 46:1). You don't have to drown when you have the God who calmed the storms, the God who healed the sick, and the God who raised the dead with you in your boat. He is a very present help. That means He is always there.

> **We add a lot of stress to our lives when Jesus becomes our last resort.**

Let God be your first resort, not your final resort. He's just waiting to hear you call His name. 90% of Christians think they're waiting on God, but in reality, He is waiting on them.

Reflection:

Spend some time today praying and asking God for help in certain areas of your life where you feel like you're drowning. Let Him calm the storms in your life.

Day 12
The Desires of Your Heart

> Psalm☐ 37:3-7☐ (ESV)
> *"Trust in the Lord, and do good; dwell in the land and befriend faithfulness. Delight yourself in the Lord, and he will give you the desires of your heart. Commit your way to the Lord; trust in him, and he will act. He will bring forth your righteousness as the light, and your justice as the noonday. Be still before the Lord and wait patiently for him; fret not yourself over the one who prospers in his way, over the man who carries out evil devices!"*

There's far too much to pull out of this passage to put into a short devotion, but I'll point out several key instructions given here. You can dig deeper into this passage afterward.

1. "Trust in the LORD." Any time we go through hard situations, "trust in the Lord" can almost become painful to hear. The phrase is often so overused by many Christians that it loses its substance. We've all tried trusting in Him, but there are times when we wonder and ask ourselves if He really has our back. It brings us more confusion than hope. Here's what the phrase doesn't mean: It doesn't mean that being a Christian makes all of your problems go away and that everything will go exactly the way you hope for

it to go. No, trusting in the LORD means that no matter what happens in my life, I'm going to thank Him and worship Him anyway. I'm going to thank him through my struggles because, whether I can see it or not, He is teaching me something and making me a stronger person through it! That's what it means to trust in Him.

2. "Delight yourself in the LORD and he will give you the desires of your heart." I remember one day, I was sitting in an ice cream shop, thinking to myself how much I was really craving a soda. Just then, a friend of mine came up to me and handed me a Mountain Dew! Now, most people would call it a coincidence, but I knew it wasn't. God sees the work I'm doing. Even though it's awfully difficult, He sees my delight in serving Him, and He gave me what my heart desired. Now, desiring a Mountain Dew is a lot smaller than desiring to be an overcomer, but God doesn't measure our desires. No matter what they are, if you delight in Him, He is willing to pull from all He owns (which is everything) and give it to those who follow Him and do it with pleasure. Loving God and loving others is the best way to gain those desires that are in your heart!

3. "Be still before the Lord and wait patiently for him." We live in a culture where everything is trying to grab your attention all at once: friends, family, school, pastors, Facebook, cell phones,

advertisements, television, video games, etc. The list never ends. With all these outside pressures, no wonder so many people are stressed out of their minds! The only way to ease that stress is to be still. Not just be still, but be still before the Lord. Silence all the outside voices, turn off the notifications, and be still. There is an overwhelming peace that comes when you are able to shut out the world and tune into God's frequency. It's in those quiet times alone with God that we're able to find that peace that surpasses all understanding. God loves spending quality time with you.

> **Peace comes when you learn to shut out the world and tune into God's frequency.**

Don't forget that there's an enemy who still wants to attack you when you try to be still. You know all those thoughts that pop in your mind at night? He reminds you of everything you forgot to do and all the stuff you have to do tomorrow. He's trying to keep your mind busy and off focus so that you can't spend that time with the only one that matters! There's real power that comes from being still.

Trust in God and He will never fail you. Delight in Him and He will give you the desires of your heart. Be still in Him and He will help you find peace.

Reflection:

Take some time to be still and shut off all the noise in your life and see how God speaks to you. Sit down with your Bible and search for His promises and let Him speak to you.

Day 13
Don't Do it Alone

This devotional is going to sound different from the rest. This one isn't as much about your relationship with God as much as it is your relationship with God's people. You're relationship with God is ultimately most important. That relationship will bring you freedom, comfort, and joy. However, your relationship with His people brings healing. The people that you hang out with directly impact your relationship with God. Why? Their influence creates you and molds you into the person you will be tomorrow.

James realized this when He wrote this passage. He

encourages you to live in relationship with His people because only there will you find healing from your lifelong struggles. If you hang out with stressed people, you're going to live anxiously. If you hang around pessimistic people, you're going to be depressed. If you hang around God's people, you're going to find peace.

Be very careful with the people you surround yourself with because they will influence the person that you become and either break down or build up strongholds in your life. Surround yourself with people who you look up to who are thriving in their walk with God. Don't find friends who claim to be Heaven, yet live like Hell. They will increase your struggles tenfold. First Corinthians 15:33 says, "Do not be deceived: Bad company ruins good morals." Choose your friends wisely. Don't let peer pressure ruin the rest of your life. The world hates the wise and praises fools. Proverbs 13:20 says, "Whoever walks with the wise becomes wise, but the companion of fools will suffer harm."

On top of this, we see the importance of confessing our sins. This passage isn't talking about quietly telling them to God, but publicly confessing them to others. That's scary... One of the main reasons that we struggle with overcoming strongholds in our lives is because we hold on to secret sin. The fear of secret sin being revealed can lead so many people into a life of loneliness and brings about more problems. However, there is no greater freedom than confiding in someone else about your sin. Secret sin is Satan's favorite stronghold. It pulls you away from God and those who love you. If you want to keep struggling, keep it to yourself. If you want freedom and lasting peace, find someone to talk to. That's where true healing begins! The more pain you store up in you, the more anxious you feel. Releasing all of that pain to the right people will bring freedom and healing!

> ## Secret sin is Satan's favorite stronghold.

Reflection:

Take some time and look over your life and who you surround yourself with. Are they bringing you closer to God or slowly pulling you away? Is it causing you more stress or less? Make the choice today to surround yourself with people, with music, and with things that will bring you closer to God and diminish the role of those who are pulling you from Him. Also, scan your heart. Is there anything in there that you're afraid for others to know? Find someone you can trust who loves God with everything, and let them know! If they have the love of Christ in them, they will feel the pain, but provide the hope and the forgiveness that you need. This alone can ease anxiety a hundredfold, and it's all birthed from God.

Day 14
Walk in the Word

2 Timothy 3:16-17 (NIV)
"All Scripture is God-breathed and is useful for teaching, rebuking, correcting and training in righteousness, so that the servant of God may be thoroughly equipped for every good work."

Joshua 1:8 (NIV)
"this book of the law shall not depart from your mouth, but you shall meditate on it day and night, so that you may be careful to do according to all that is written in it. For then you will make your way prosperous, and then you'll have good success."

Hebrews 4:12 (NIV)
"for the word of God is living and active, sharper than any two edge sword, piercing to the division of soul and spirit, joints and of narrow, and discerning the thoughts and intentions of the heart."

The Bible is not a list of do's and don'ts. It's a guidebook to our entire lives. When we are always asking God to speak, we should look into His word for truth. The Bible is the Word of God. He wrote down everything you need to know to live a life without regret and pain. God doesn't want to see us in a situation that leads to pain and anguish. That is why He gave us a guidebook.

People all over the world, even Christians, tend to blame God for their circumstances even though He has already given them clear instruction in His Word of how to avoid them. I always get prayer requests from people who don't realize that their struggles won't go away by praying, but applying biblical principles to their lives. What most people need is not more prayer, but more knowledge of the Bible. Our spiritual growth will never exceed our knowledge of the Bible.

> **Your spiritual growth will never exceed your knowledge of scripture.**

The Bible says, "as His divine power has given to us all things that *pertain* to life and godliness, through the knowledge of Him who called us by glory and virtue" (2 Pet. 1:3). Some of life's most common strongholds are brought on by our own choices and our own circumstances. The thought, "I don't know what to do" can lead us into a whirlwind emotionally, physically, and spiritually. The book of proverbs continually encourages us to seek wisdom in the Word so that we know what to do when these times come and so we can prepare ourselves in advance to avoid certain pains and struggles.

The Bible has information about almost every area of your life: marriage, money management, prayer, relationship building, and much more. You have a question, the Bible is very likely to hold the answer. You just have to read it and know it.

Most Christians neglect this part of their relationship with Jesus, even though this is probably the most important. Don't let that be you.

God has so much He wants to show you in His Word. He wants to light up the path that you're on. He wants to share with you how much you are loved. He wants to show you a way out! You can only find that in his Word.

Final Reflection:
This is the last devotional of this book, but this is just a taste of what you can get when you study the Bible personally. This book is full of Biblical principles that can help guide you into facing and defeating any stronghold in your life. I could write countless devotionals and books regarding this topic, but they will all come from the pages of Scripture. Spend time every day getting to know your Creator better. Look for the truth that's written in the pages of God's word and let Him transform your mind. When He transforms your mind, He transforms your heart. When He transforms your heart, He transforms your entire life!